STOCK MARKET TERMINOLOGY FOR BEGINNERS

A Complete Guide to Learning the Stock Market Lingo

Christopher Hamilton

TABLE OF CONTENTS

Book Description

A re you thinking of trading stocks? Do you have the interest and enthusiasm to trade stocks but lack basic knowledge and understanding of basic stock terminologies?

Well, you have come to the right place!

Even though stock investing does not require a lot of money and time, you must be willing to equip yourself with basic tools and the necessary training to help you make the right decisions. Think about it – what is the most well-known metric for measuring a country's economy? Maybe it is the strength of its currency, right?

However, this can be greatly influenced by speculators and liquidity. Before investing in the stock market, you must familiarize yourself with basic stock terminologies. Think of it as learning to speak a new language. If you ask any seasoned stock investor, they will tell you they started by learning the investing terms.

There's no need to panic because it will not take long. Once you are done reading this book, you will start speaking the stock investing language in no time. Here, we will break down some essential stock terms every investor must know to invest their money wisely!

So, what are you still waiting for?

Take a deep breath, relax, and learn!

Introduction

Look around you – you will realize that most people turn to the country's stock market performance to indicate how well the economy is doing. The truth is, stock markets cover all industries in all sectors of the economy. This simply means the stock market is a barometer that tells you which cycle of the economy we are in and the hopes and fears of the population generating wealth and growth.

This book is for anyone who wants to learn the terms within the stock market. These terms are not just making you sound cool but are relevant in the stock market and will help you know what to look for. There is a lot of fluff or stock market lingo that isn't really needed to understand a good stock. Therefore, I have created this book to give you the terms that matter and save you a lot of time trying and figuring out these terms independently.

Learning stocks can seem overwhelmingly difficult, but in this book, I will give the terms and define them for you to have a guide you can always refer to. Research the terms, come back to this book, share with your friends, whatever you may do, at least you know you're searching for terms that matter as a beginner.

Before we delve deeper into the key terminologies used in the stock market, let's first understand the meaning of the stock market and how it works.

The stock market is a collection of markets and exchanges where buying, selling, and issuing publicly-held company shares happen. These activities happen through institutionalized formal exchanges or over-the-counter marketplaces operating under a set of regulations.

Perhaps you are thinking, *"is there a difference between the stock market and stock exchanges?"*

Yes, there is a difference!

While most people use these terms interchangeably, the stock exchange is a subset of the stock market. If you say you trade in the stock market, it simply means you buy and sell shares or equities on one or more of the stock exchanges, which are part of the overall stock market. Some of the leading stock exchanges in the US are Nasdaq, New York Stock Exchange (NYSE), and Chicago Board Options Exchange (CBOE). All these stock exchanges make up the US's stock market.

Think about it – people drive to the city's outskirts and farmlands to buy a Christmas tree. You will likely drive to the timber market if you want wood for home furniture or renovations. If you need groceries, you will likely go to the stores like Walmart to get them.

In short, there are dedicated markets where buyers and sellers come to interact and transact. The best part is that you are assured of fair prices because many market participants are large. For instance, if you only have one seller of Christmas trees in the entire city, he has the freedom to charge whatever prices he wants because the buyers don't have anywhere else to go. However, if the number of Christmas tree sellers is large in the same marketplace, they will have to compete to attract buyers.

The same thing happens when shopping online – you will compare prices offered by different sellers on the same or across different shopping portals to get the best deals. This forces online sellers to offer competitive prices.

You have the same designated market for trading various stocks in a controlled, secure and well-managed environment in the stock market. The stock market brings together many market participants who want to buy or sell shares, ensuring fair pricing and transaction transparency. In the past, stock markets dealt in paper-based physical share certificates. Today, the stock market deals in computer-aided stock markets operating electronically.

Stock markets offer the best option for you to invest your money. In other words, setting aside money while you are busy with life and then having that money work for you so that you can fully reap the fruits of your labor. I like to think of investing as a means to a happy future. According to Warren Buffet, investing means *"…laying out money now to receive more money in the future."*

Think about it – if you have $1000 to set aside, you are ready to invest in the stock market. When you invest in this way, you earmark money for the future, hoping it will grow over time. Stock trading offers you – *especially beginners* – the opportunity to gain an investment experience.

Before you commit your money to stock investment, you must ask yourself, *"what kind of investor am I?"*

Think about your investment goals and how much risk you are willing to take. While there are investors who wish to take an active hand in managing the growth of their money, there are those who choose to set it aside and forget it. The good news is that the stock market offers you a secure and regulated environment where you can transact in shares and other eligible financial instruments with a high degree of confidence.

The most important thing to note is that the stock market acts both as a;

Primary market
Secondary market

Primary market – simply means that the stock market allows companies to issue and sell their shares to the public for the first time by issuing initial public offerings (IPO) at a set price – like $20/share.

To facilitate this process, the company will need a marketplace to sell, and the stock market provides this. The stock exchange facilitates and gets a fee for its services from the company and its financial partners during the capital raising process.

Secondary market – Following the first-time issuance of IPO – also referred to as the listing process – the stock exchange acts as a trading platform for regular trading – buying and selling. This is referred to as secondary market activity taking place in a secondary market. The stock exchange is responsible for maintaining price discovery, liquidity, price transparency, and fair-trading activities.

The stock exchange also offers additional shares through follow-on offers, rights issues, or even buybacks and facilitates such transactions. It also creates and maintains a wide range of market-level and sector-specific indicators that help you track the movements in the overall market. Additionally, the stock exchanges maintain company announcements, news, and financial reporting accessible through their official websites.

PART 1: ON THE SURFACE

Stock price

This refers to the current price a stock share is trading for in the stock market. When the shares of a publicly-traded company are issued, they are assigned value that ideally reflects its value. The stock prices may go up or down depending on industry changes, environmental changes, war, changes in the economy, or political events.

One mistake people make is assuming that when the stock price is low, it means they are cheap, and when the stock price is high, it means they are expensive. The truth is, stock prices tell very little about the stock's value. Most importantly, it does not predict whether the value is headed higher or lower. Your main goal as a stock investor is to identify stocks currently undervalued by the market.

Let's consider an example – one company has created a game-changing technology while another is laying off staff to cut down on cost. What stocks would you want to buy?

It helps to dig deeper instead of "judging a book by the cover." You might be surprised that the company that has just created a game-changing technology does not have a plan to build its initial success. On the other hand, the company cutting costs may already be streamlining its operations to achieve success.

The stock prices only tell you the current value of a company or its market value. If there are more buyers than sellers, the chances are that the stock prices will rise, and vice versa. Your role is to investigate the company to determine its true value.

Ticker symbol

This is a unique string of letters assigned to security for trading. For instance, stocks listed on the NYSE might have four letters or fewer. On the other hand, those listed on the Nasdaq may be up to five letters. For example, if you wanted to search for Amazon, you would simply type in AMZN, or for Nike, it would be NKE. These symbols are just a shorthand way of describing stocks by different **companies.**

When a company issues their securities to the public marketplace, they select symbols for their shares – often related to the company's name. The investors and traders will then use these symbols to place trade orders. There is no significant difference between those with three letters and those with four or five. Additional letters simply mean the stocks have more features like trading restrictions or share class, ranging between A and Z.

But what happens if the company has more than one class of shares trading in the market?

In that case, it adds a class to its suffix. For instance, preferred stocks called Jeff's Tequila Corporate preferred A shares would use the symbol JTC.PR.A.

If a company is in a bankruptcy proceeding, it will have a Q letter after its symbol. On the other hand, if the company is non-US but is trading in the US financial markets, it will have a Y letter following its ticker symbol. **Stocks**

Think about it – when you purchase a company's stocks, you purchase a small portion of that company called a share. Therefore, stocks are defined as securities that represent your ownership share in a company. As an investor, if you think that a company's stocks will grow in value, you can purchase a slice of that company and sell your shares later for a profit. They are ways for you to grow your money and outpace inflation.

There are two types of stocks: common stocks and preferred stocks.

Common stocks

Are you new to stock investing? Are you looking to buy a few shares?

If yes, then you might want to invest in common stocks. As the name suggests, common stocks refer to the most common type of stock in the market. When you own common stocks, it simply means you own a slice of the company's profits and the right to vote. You may also earn dividends, which is regularly a payment made to you – the stock owner. However, these dividends are typically variable and not a guarantee you will receive them.

Pros

> They offer you potential for higher long-term returns
> You have voting rights

Cons

> The dividends – if available – are variable, lower, and not guaranteed
> Their prices are highly volatile
> In case the company goes bankrupt, you risk losing your investment

Preferred stocks

Preferred stock is the type of stock in which you are entitled to a fixed dividend whose payment is prioritised over ordinary share dividends. They have a higher claim on distribution compared to common stocks.

Pros

> The dividends are higher, fixed, and guaranteed
> Their prices are less volatile
> In the event of a liquidation, you are likely to recover at least part of your investment

Cons

> In most cases, you have limited or no voting rights in corporate governance.
> You have a lower long-term potential for growth.

Basis point

This refers to a unit of measure used in finance to describe the % change in the rate or value of a financial instrument. It is also denoted as bps or "bips." 1 bps = 0.01%. Bps describes the yield a bond pays to an investor in the bond market.

Investors commonly use bips to describe the incremental interest rate change for securities and interest rate reporting. Additionally, they are used to prevent ambiguity or confusion when talking about absolute and relative interest rates – especially in cases where the rate difference is less than a percent, but the amount has a material significance.

Percent

This refers to the number of points divided into the value of the stock, which produces a percentage change.

Let us consider an example;

If you say that a company's stocks are up 5 points from $100/share, it simply means it's up to $5, which translates to a 5% gain. In short, the percent value is always calculated from the starting value, which makes the comparison understandable.

Types of charts

As an investor, you must first understand that technical analysis is about timing. While a stock may be doing very well, you risk incurring heavy losses if you trade at the wrong price. This explains why traders use a wide range of tools to make informed decisions in the stock market. The biggest tool is the stock chart.

When performing technical analysis, there are three major principles you must bear in mind;

Stock prices reflect all the relevant information about the market
The stock prices move with market trends
History has a way of repeating itself

If the stock prices move in patterns, the trick is to study the patterns to help you make informed trading decisions, hence the reason you must learn to use stock charts – graphical representations of stock volume and price movements over a certain duration. Typically, the X-axis represents the time – which varies from intra-day to months or more – while the Y-axis represents the movement in price.

There are various types of charts;

Line chart

This is the most common type of chart that tracks the stock's closing prices over a specific duration. A dot represents every closing price, and all the dots are connected by lines, which give a graphical representation. While most people think of the line chart as simplistic, traders can use it to spot trends in price movements.

Bar chart

This is quite similar to the line chart, except it offers more information. Instead of a dot, every plot point is represented by a vertical line with two horizontal lines from both sides. The top part of the vertical line is the highest price at which a stock is traded during the day. On the other hand, the lower part is the lowest traded price. The extension on the left represents the price at which the stock opened. While on the right represents the closing price for the day.

The bar chart also offers insight into volatility. For instance, if the line is longer, it simply means greater volatility in trading the stocks.

Candlestick charts

These charts are popular among technical analysts because they precisely offer a lot of information. As the name suggests, the movement in stock price is represented in candlestick shape. The bar chart has 4 data points – high, low, open, and close. However, this chart gives volatility information for a longer period, and the price movements are represented in different colors. A falling stick is black or red, while a rising candlestick is white or clear.

That said, as you trade in the stock market, you must read the chart and understand the information it represents to help you identify patterns in price movements and use that to make informed trading decisions.

Time frame

This is the amount of time a trend lasts in the stock market and can be identified and used by traders. These trends can be classified as primary, intermediate, or short-term. The truth is, markets can exist in several time frames simultaneously. In that case, there can be conflicting trends within a stock depending on the time frame considered. It is not unusual to find stocks on a primary uptrend while mired in the short-term or intermediate downtrends.

A general rule of thumb is that the signals are more reliable when the time frame is longer. The more you drill down in the time frames, the more polluted the charts with noises and false moves. Ideally, it would be best to use a longer time frame to define the primary trends of whatever stocks you are trading.

Range

This displays how many periods you wish to display, which is a key depending on the information you want. Looking at the stock charts, you can tell where prices have been for a particular duration without much description. Once you set the range, you can tell the stock movement for that time. There are various default settings – like *1,5 or 10 days; 1,3 or 6 months; 1,3,5,or 10 years.*

Watchlist

These are securities monitored for their potential in trading or as investment opportunities. Just as the name suggests, it is a list of stocks an investor watches with the aim of leveraging price falls to create interesting undervalued situations. With several instruments, you can create a watchlist to help you make informed and timely investment decisions. You can also use a watchlist to keep track of companies and keep up with financial events and news that could impact these instruments.

Bid and ask

Bid and ask are also referred to as bid and offer. They refer to two-way price quotations indicating the best possible price a security can be bought and sold at a certain time. The bid price is the maximum price a buyer is willing to pay for a share of stock or securities. On the other hand, the asking price is the minimum price a seller is willing to take for that specific security. A buyer must be willing to pay the best offer available or sell at the highest bid for a transaction to happen.

The difference between the bid and ask is the spread, which gives information on liquidity; in other words, the smaller the spread, the greater the liquidity of that security.

For instance, if the current price for a stock of ABC is $12.50 / $12.55, if you are looking to buy A at the current market price, you will pay $12.55, while another investor who wishes to sell ABC shares at the current market price will receive $12.50.

Volume

This refers to the number of assets or securities changing hands over a given period, in most cases for the day. For example, the stock trading volume would be the number of shares of security traded between daily open and close. Generally, stocks with more daily volume are considered more liquid than those without because they are more active.

In technical analysis, volume is a key indicator used to measure the relative significance of a market move. If the volume is higher during a price move, the move is considered more significant. However, if the volume is lower during a price move, then the move is considered less significant.

In short, volume tells you more about the market activity and liquidity. Suppose you feel hesitant about the stock market direction; in that case, the chances are that future trading volumes will likely increase, causing options and futures ion-specific stocks to trade actively. Overall, volumes tend to be higher near the market's opening and closing times; and on Mondays and Fridays. Additionally, they are lower during lunchtimes and before holiday seasons.

Previous close

This is a security's – including stock, commodity, bond, futures or options contract, or market index – closing price of the preceding time of the one being referenced. Almost always, it refers to the previous day's final price of a security when the market officially closed for the day.

It is an important daily metric used for reporting purposes in financial information. It marks the daily measuring point against which updated returns are calculated, and new information is collected to inform new decisions and strategies. It is one of two key components in a candlestick day chart.

Today's open

This is the starting period of trading on a security exchange or organized over the counter market. In most cases, an order is considered open until the client cancels it, is executed, or expires. Depending on the exchange, today's open can be the first executed trade price for that specific day. However, there is a good chance that the open price may not be the same as the previous day's closing price.

You must note that different exchanges have different opening times. For instance, NYSE may open at 9:30 am EST, while CME may open at 7:20 am CST. That said, the main reason an order may remain open is that it carries such conditions as stop levels or price limits. The other reason may be a lack of liquidity for that specific security. In other words, if there are no established bids and offers by market makers, it means no trading will happen.

Market cap

This is also referred to as market capitalization. It is the total dollar market value of a company's outstanding shares of stock. To calculate the market cap, you multiply the total number of the company's outstanding shares by the current market share price.

Let us consider an example; A company X has 10 million shares selling for $100/share with a market cap of $1 billion. In that case, investors will use this figure to tell the company size instead of using total asset figures or sales. In an acquisition, the market cap will determine whether a takeover candidate is a good value or not to the party acquiring it. The initial market cap of a company is established through an IPO. Before that, the company that wishes to go public must enlist an investment bank to employ valuation techniques to help derive a company's value and determine how many shares will be offered to the public and at what price.

Once the company goes public and begins trading on the exchange, the share price is determined based on supply and demand in the market. The price will likely increase if the demand is high due to favorable factors. However, if the company's future growth potential is in doubt, the sellers will likely drive the price down. In that case, the market cap becomes a real-time estimate of the company's value.

Market cap = share price x # shares outstanding

1-year target estimate

This refers to the predicted price of stocks a year from the current date. In most cases, the price levels reflect the analysts' collective opinion on where they think the stocks will be trading a year from now. For analysts to estimate, they must predict what a company's business will be like in a year by focusing on the revenue and other key factors. Additionally, they must consider the investor's willingness to pay a given price. That said, the results of such predictions are usually not extremely successful.

Average volume

This refers to the average number of shares you trade within a day in a given stock. While daily volume is the number of shares you trade each day, averaging this over several days gives you the average daily volume. The average volume is a key metric because high or low trading volumes attract different traders and investors.

Most traders and investors prefer high trading volumes compared to lower volumes. This is mainly because high volumes are easier to get into and out of position. On the contrary, lower volumes have fewer buyers and sellers, making it harder to enter or exit at the most desired price.

Higher volumes indicate that the securities you are trading are highly competitive, have narrower spreads, and are less volatile. Does this mean they will not have large price moves? Definitely not! Any stock can have a huge price move on any day, even higher than average volume.

You can use the average volume as a metric for analyzing the price action of liquid assets. In other words, if the price of an asset is rangebound and a breakout happens, an increase in volume is likely to confirm the breakout. However, a lack of volume indicates that a breakout will likely fail.

Dividend yield

This refers to a financial ratio of dividends/price showing how much a company pays out in dividends annually relative to its stock price. This value is expressed as a percentage. Manufacture companies likely pay dividend yield, while those with higher dividend yields are likely to be in the utility and consumer staple industries.

Even though companies in the REITs, BDCs, and MLPs are thought to pay higher than average dividends, they are taxed heavily. This is why investors must bear in mind that higher dividend yields don't always mean an attractive investment opportunity because the dividends of a stock might be increased because of a decline in stock price.

Earnings date

This is the date of the next release of a company's financial report. This is when the company's profitability for a particular duration is officially announced. In most cases, companies in the private sector must give quarterly financial reports to stock exchanges across the world so that investors know the company's state.

Percentage change

This is a mathematical concept representing the extent of change happening over time. In finance, this is important in telling a security's price change. This value can be applied to any quantity you measure over time. For instance, if you are tracking the quoted price of a security, a price increase is calculated using the following formula; [(New Price - Old Price)/Old Price] x 100.

If the answer you get is a negative value, it simply means the percentage change is a decrease.

Alternatively, a price decrease is calculated using the formula; [(Old Price - New Price)/Old Price] x 100.

If the answer you get is a negative value, it simply means the percentage change is an increase.

52 weeks high and low

This refers to a data point in data feeds obtained from online financial information sources, including the lowest and highest price at which a stock has traded for 52 weeks. Most investors use this kind of information to tell how much fluctuation or risk they have to endure over a year if they choose to invest in a particular stock.

The 52-week range can be obtained from stock's quote summary by brokers or financial information websites. You can also see the visual representation on a price chart displaying one year's worth of price data. Considering that price movement is not always balanced or symmetrical, investors must know the most recent number – the high or the low. In most cases, the number closest to the current price is assumed to be the most recent. However, this is not always the case. That said, not having the correct information risks making costly investment decisions.

Shares outstanding

These are the number of stocks present in an open market held by its shareholders, institutional investors, company officers, and insiders. On a balance sheet, they are termed as Capital stock. A share outstanding is used in calculating key metrics like market cap, earning per share, and cash flow per share. This number is not static and is likely to fluctuate wildly over time.

Analyst ratings

This refers to a measure of a stock's expected performance over a given duration. In most cases, analysts and brokerage firms use these ratings when issuing stock recommendations to traders. The analysts arrive at these ratings after conducting comprehensive research into the public financial statements of different companies, talking to customers and executives, or attending conferences.

These ratings are issued at least four times annually – once every quarter. Target prices accompany these analyst ratings to help traders gain deeper insight into a stock's fair prices than the current market value. There are different types of ratings;

Buy rating is a recommendation to buy specific stocks. It implies that an analyst expects the stock price to rise short- or mid-term.

Sell rating is a recommendation to sell specific stocks. It implies that the analyst expects the stock prices to decline below the current short- and mid-term levels. This means the analyst has identified key challenges in the company.

Hold rating implies that an analyst expects that the stock will perform in line with the market at the same pace as similar stock. It tells brokers not to sell their stock nor buy more. Often, this rating is given when a company is not sure whether or not it will meet its guidance even though it's making respectable profits.

Underperform rating implies that a company's stock is likely worse than the market average or the benchmark index. In that case, traders are advised to stay away from the stock. This is often expected when a company's growth slugs more than the previous quarter.

Outperform rating implies a stock is expected to yield higher returns than the benchmark index or market average. Typically, this rating says that this is a good buying opportunity for a particular stock.

That said, it is your responsibility as a trader or investor to do your due diligence because analyst ratings are just a starting point but are far from fail-proof.

ETFS

This refers to a set of securities that track a specific set of equities. They trade the same way stocks do, and just like an index, they track equities. Investors who purchase shares of ETFs gain exposure to a basket of equities ad limited company-specific risks associated with a single stock, hence offering them cost-effective ways to diversify their portfolio.

PART 2: UNDER THE SURFACE

Enterprise value (EV)

This refers to the measure of a company's overall value. This metric is often used as a comprehensive alternative to equity market cap.

To calculate EV, use the formula:

EV = MC + Total Debt – C

Where:

MC is the market capitalization, equal to the current stock price multiplied by outstanding stock shares.

Total debt is the sum of both short- and long-term debts.

C is the cash and its equivalents, including its liquid assets and not the marketable securities.

If the market cap is not readily available, multiply the number of outstanding shares by the current stock price.

Perhaps you are thinking, *"what does EV tell me?"*

Think of the EV as the theoretical takeover price of the company were to be bought. This is different from a simple market cap in various ways and may be considered an accurate representation of the firm's value. For instance, the buyer must pay the value of a company's debt when they take over the company. Hence, EV offers a more accurate takeover valuation because it factors debt in calculating value.

So, why doesn't the market cap accurately represent a company's value?

The truth is, the market cap leaves out some of the most important factors like company debt and cash reserves. In that case, EV serves as a modification of the market cap because it incorporates these factors when determining a company's total value. This explains why EV is popularly used as a basis for many financial ratios measuring a company's performance.

That said, before you use the EV formula, you must beware of its downsides. Knowing EV considers the total debt, you must consider how the company has used this debt. For instance, in capital-intensive companies, businesses tend to shoulder a huge amount of debt, which is used to spur growth. Therefore, while EV calculation may be skewed against these companies in favor of companies in low/zero debt industries, you will likely miss the bigger picture if you rely solely on EV.

EBITDA

This refers to a measure of a company's ability to generate revenue. This is majorly used as an alternative to net income or simple earnings in certain situations. To calculate EBITDA, use the formula:

EBITDA = recurring earnings from continuing operations + interest + taxes + depreciation + amortization

That said, this value can be quite misleading because it strips out the cost of capital investment – like equipment, property, or plant. In that case, you can choose to use EBIT. This similar financial metric does not have the downside of eliminating depreciation and amortization expenses associated with equipment, property, and plant. When EV and EBITDA are combined, you get a valuation tool that efficiently compares a company's value – including debt – to a company's cash earnings – minus non-cash expenses. This is ideal for analysts seeking to compare companies within the same industry.

That said, EBITDA has several drawbacks;

First, in cases where the working capital is growing, this metric will overstate the cash flows from operations. It will also ignore how different revenue recognition policies affect its operations cash flow. Secondly, considering that free cash flows to the company capture the number of capital expenditures, it is highly linked with the valuation theory than EBITDA, which typically is an adequate measure if capital expenses are the same as depreciation expenses.

Trailing and forward p/e

The price-to-earnings ratio, the P/E ratio, is a metric that compares the price of a company's stock to the earnings generated by the company. This comparison plays a critical role in helping one understand whether the markets are undervaluing or overvaluing stocks.

To obtain the P/E ratio, simply divide the stock price by the stock's earnings.

I like to think of it this way – the market price of a stock tells you how much people are willing to pay to own shares. However, the P/E ratio will tell you whether the price accurately reflects a company's earning potential or its value over time.

Let us consider an example – if a company's stocks are trading at $50 per share and the company generates $5/share in annual earnings, then the P/E ratio of the company's stocks would be (50/5), which equals 10. In other words, given the company's current earnings, it would take ten years for the accumulated earnings to equal the investment cost.

Considering that prices keep fluctuating, it is safe to say that the P/E ratio of stocks and stock indices never standstill. This value also changes as the company reports earnings – typically, every quarter.

There are two variants of the P/E ratio;

Trailing P/E ratio

This is a measure of the EPS of stocks for the past 12 months. To calculate this value, use the formula;

Trailing P/E ratio = Current per share price of a stock/EPS from the previous year

This ratio accounts for a company's actual earnings rather than its projected earnings, hence why it is considered the most accurate way of determining its value. The trailing P/E ratio offers a fair stock valuation in a perfect market.

Forward P/E ratio

This metric forecasts a company's likely earnings per share for the next 12 months.

Forward P/E ratio = Stock's current share price / future earnings

The difference between the trailing and forward P/E ratios is that the former is based on actual performance stats while the latter is based on performance estimates.

Determining the P/E ratio is specifically important to investors because it reveals what is paid per dollar that a company logs in its bottom line. If an investor can tap into the profits for a fairly low price, a clear bargain must be obtained. However, if the cost is high compared to the earnings, you must ask why.

The good thing about the forward P/E ratio is that it helps a company compare its present earnings to those already on track to make in the future. Investors must pay close attention to the forward-looking indicators as new figures trickle in. The only downside is that most investors try to beat the system by claiming higher earnings at first and then adjusting the figure towards the next announcements. Alternatively, they claim lower earnings figures in one quarter to ensure that the next quarter beats their estimates.

Peg ratio

Peg ratio stands for price/earnings to growth ratio. It refers to a stock's P/E ratio divided by the growth rate of its earnings over a specific duration. This ratio is used to determine the value of stocks considering a company's expected earnings growth. Most analysts believe that the peg ratio offers a complete picture than the standard P/E ratio we discussed earlier.

To calculate the Peg ratio, use the formula:

PEG ratio = EPS growth price / EPS

Where EPS stands for earnings per share.

Like any ratio, the accuracy of the peg ratio depends on the inputs used. If considering using a company's peg ratio from a publication, you must determine the growth rate used in the calculation. Realize that using historical growth rates tends to give an inaccurate PEG ratio if you anticipate that the growth rate will change in the future.

While a low P/E ratio tends to make a stock look like a good buy, incorporating a company's growth rate in calculating the peg ratio tells a different story. The lower the peg ratio, the higher the chances of undervalued stocks, given future earnings expectations. You adjust the results by adding a company's expected growth rate, especially if the company has a high growth rate and a high P/E ratio.

Price to sales

This is a valuation ratio comparing its stock price to its revenues. It serves as an indicator of the company's value that financial markets have placed on every dollar of its revenues or sales.

This ratio demonstrates how much investors are willing to pay per dollar of sales. To calculate it, you can either divide the company's market cap by the total sales over 12 months; or calculate it on a per-share basis by dividing the stock price by the sales per share. The P/S ratio is also known as revenue - or sales multiple.

Like any other ratio, the P/S ratio is relevant when comparing companies within the same industry/sector. When the ratio is low, it means the stocks are undervalued. However, if it is significantly above average, it may suggest stock overvaluation.

To calculate the P/S ratio, use the formula;

P/S ratio = MVS / SPS

Where:

MVS is the market value per share, and SPS
is the sales per share.

That said, the P/S ratio does not consider whether a company makes any earnings or will ever make any earnings in the future. Therefore, comparing companies in different sectors can be pretty difficult. For instance, a company that makes video games has different capabilities of turning profits than a company that deals with groceries. Additionally, this metric does not account for the company's balance sheet status for debt loads. A company with virtually no debt is considered more attractive than highly leveraged, even if the P/S ratios are the same.

Price to book (P/B ratio)

This is one of the most widely used financial ratios that compare a company's market price to its book value. In other words, the P/B ratio shows the value given by the market for every dollar of a company's net worth. In most high-growth companies, their P/B ratios tend to be above 1.0. On the other hand, those facing severe distress tend to have P/B ratios below 1.0.

To calculate the P/B ratio, use the formula:

P/B ratio = Market price per share / Book value per share

The company's book value refers to the tangible net asset value calculated by subtracting intangible assets from total assets – like goodwill and patents. If the P/B ratio is low, it suggests that the stock is undervalued. It could also mean that something is fundamentally amiss with the company. Just like most ratios, the P/B ratio varies across industries. It also indicates that you are paying too much for what would remain if the company is declared bankrupt.

This metric reflects the value market participants attach to a company's equity relative to the equity's book value. While the stock's market value is a forward-looking metric of a company's projected cash flows, the book value is based on the cost principle. It mirrors the past issuance of equity, augmented by losses or profits and reduced by share buybacks and dividends.

If a company is liquidated and all its debts paid, the remaining value would be its book value. In other words, it offers a reality check for investors looking for growth at a reasonable price. It is looked at concerning the return on equity (ROE), a reliable growth indicator.

STOCKMARKETTERMINOLOGYFORBEGINNERS | **37**

Let us consider an example – assuming a company has $150 million in assets and $100 million liabilities. The company's book value would be ($150-$80), which equals $50. If $10 million shares are outstanding, each share will represent $5.00 of the book value. If the share price is $10, the P/B ratio would be 2 x (10/5).

That said, if the accounting standards used by companies differ, the P/B ratio is likely to be non-comparable, especially in cases where the companies are in different countries. This metric may also be less useful for companies with little tangible assets on their balance sheet. Additionally, this value can be negative because of a long series of negative earnings, making it useless for relative valuation.

50-day and 200-day moving average

A moving average refers to an arithmetic mean of many data points. A 50-day moving average is the sum of the past 50 data points divided by 50. On the other hand, a 200-day moving average is the sum of the past 200 data points divided by 200.

Therefore, the difference between these two moving averages is the number of periods used in their calculation. Many technical traders use these moving averages to help them choose whether to enter or exit a position, making these levels strong support or resistance measures.

You must note that moving averages are often viewed as low-risk areas to set a transaction because they correspond to the average price a trader is paid over a specific duration. For instance, a 50-day moving average equals all investors' average price to obtain assets over ten weeks. Similarly, a 200-day moving average equals the average price over 40 weeks.

Once the prices fall below these averages, it acts as a resistance. Mainly, this is because individuals who have taken a position may consider closing their position to avoid suffering a significant loss.

Held by insiders

Insider is a term used to describe senior officers or directors of a publicly-traded company. It is also used to describe any entity that beneficially owns more than 10% of a company's voting shares or has non-public knowledge. The thing with insiders is that they must comply with strict disclosure requirements regarding the purchase or sale of a company's shares.

In the US, the Securities and Exchange Commission (SEC) makes the rules about insider trading. Insider trading is not always an illegal activity as insiders can legally sell, buy, or trade stocks in their company if they notify SEC.

According to SEC, an insider is any investor that gains insider information through their work as officers, corporate directors, or employees of a company. If these people share information with their friends, family, or business associates, and they go ahead and exchange stocks in the company, they are termed, insiders. Insider trading is considered a violation of trust investors place in the stock market because it undermines fairness in investing.

Held by institutions

This is also termed institutional ownership. It refers to the amount of a company's available stocks owned by insurance companies, pension funds, mutual funds, private foundations, investment firms, or endowments, among other large entities managing funds on others' behalf.

In most instances, stocks held by institutions are considered favorable. Large institutions often employ a team of analysts who perform comprehensive and costly financial research before purchasing a large block of a company's stock, making the decision influential to potential investors.

After considering the investment made in research, most institutions are not quick to sell their position. When they do, it is often viewed as a judgment on the value of the stock, which drives down their prices. On the other hand, institutions may drive the share prices high once they own the stock through TV adverts, presentations, and articles in high-profile publications or investor conferences, which ultimately move the stock higher and thus increase the value of their position.

Realize that when an institution represents a majority of ownership in a given security, several issues may arise. With the available resources, these entities can control almost all outstanding security shares. This concentration of ownership contributes to peak ownership with little room for new retail investors or reasonable trading activities.

Payout ratio

This is a financial metric that shows the proportion of earnings a company pays its shareholders as dividends, also called the dividend payout ratio. This payout ratio is expressed as a percentage of a company's total earnings.

This metric is often used in determining a company dividend payment program's sustainability. Typically, a higher payout ratio – of over 100% - means more sustainability. Conversely, a lower payout ratio suggests that a company chooses to reinvest a significant amount of its earnings in expanding operations. Historically, if a company has the best long-term dividend payment records, its payout ratios are considered stable over time.

To calculate the payout ratio, use the formula:

DPR = Total dividends / Net income

That said, no single number defines the ideal DPR mainly because its adequacy depends largely on the industry/sector in which a company operates. In most cases, companies operating in defensive sectors boast stable earnings and cash flow able to support high payouts over a long duration. However, companies that make less reliable payouts face macroeconomic fluctuations that make their profits vulnerable.

Ex-dividend date

This is also referred to as the ex-date. It is the day stocks start trading without their next dividend payment value. Typically, this is one business day before the record date. This means that an investor buying stocks on its ex-date or later is not eligible to receive the declared dividends. In other words, the dividend payment is made to the person or entity that owned stocks a day before the ex-date. The ex-date happens before the record date because a stock trade is settled 'T+1', which means that transaction's record is not settled for one business day.

For instance, if an investor owned the stock on Thursday, January 14 but sold them on Friday, January 15, they are considered the shareholder of record on Monday, January 18, because the trade has not fully settled. However, if the investor sold on Thursday, January 14, the trade would have settled on Friday, January 15, before the record date of Monday, January 18; and the new buyer would be entitled to receiving the dividend payment.

If your investment strategy is focused on income, you must know when the ex-date happens to plan your trade entries better. That said, considering the stock price declines by about the same value of dividends, buying the stock just before the ex-date should not result in any profits. Similarly, investors who buy stocks on the ex-date or after a discount are not entitled to dividends.

Fiscal year-end

This refers to completing any 12-months accounting time other than a typical calendar year. Once a company chooses its fiscal-year end, often when they incorporate or form a company, it must stick with year after year to allow for consistency of accounting data concerning time frame. If a company's fiscal year-end is the same as its calendar year-end, it means the fiscal year ends on 31 December.

That said, every company can choose the best fiscal yearend based on their needs. Annually, every public company must publish its financial statements to be reviewed by SEC. These documents play a critical role in updating investors on the company's performance compared to previous years. It also offers analysts a better understanding of the company's business operations. These financial statements are published after the company's fiscal yearend, which differs from one company to another.

Fiscal year

This refers to a one-year duration in which companies and governments do financial budgeting and reporting. In most cases, the fiscal year is used to prepare financial statements. Even though a fiscal year can begin on the 1st of January and end on the 31st of December, not every fiscal year corresponds with the calendar year.

Think about it – a college often starts and ends their fiscal year based on the school year, right?

In the case of publicly traded companies and their investors, it serves as a time when revenues and earnings are measured, making year-to-year comparisons possible. A company may choose to report its financial information on a non-calendar fiscal year, depending on the nature of its revenue cycle.

Profit margin

This is a profitability ratio that measures the extent to which a company or business makes money. In other words, it is a representation of a company's sales that are turned into profits. For instance, if a company reports a 40% profit margin in the previous quarter, it means its net income was $0.40 of every dollar of sales generated.

There are four levels of profit margins; operating profits, gross profits, net profits, and pre-tax profits. All these are reflected in a company's income statements in this order; a company takes in sales revenue and pays direct costs of their products or services and is left with gross margins. After that, it pays indirect costs and is left with an operating margin. Then it pays interest on debt, adds unusual inflows or minuses charges, and is left with a pre-tax margin. It then pays taxes and is left with a net margin, also termed net income as its bottom line.

Profit margin is a key indicator of a company's financial health, growth potential, and management skills. While the profit margins vary from one sector to another, caution must be taken when comparing the figures for different companies and businesses.

To calculate the profit margin, use the formula;

Profit margin = 1 – (Expenses / Net Sales)

Let us consider an example;

If a company generates sales worth $200,000 by spending $100,000, the profit margin would be [1 – ($100,000/$200,000)], which equals 50%. If the cost of generating the same sales declines to $50,000, it means the profit margin shoots to [1 – ($50,000/$200,000), which equals 75%.

In short, when cost declines, the profit margin increases. Therefore, to improve the profit margin, a company must reduce costs and increase sales. Theoretically, increasing sales can be achieved by increasing the volume of units sold, increasing the prices, or both. That said, a price increase should only happen to the extent to which a company does not lose its competitive edge in the marketplace.

Operating margin

This measures how much profit a company makes on a dollar of sales once it pays for the variable cost of production before paying interest or tax. In short;

Operating margin = Operating earnings / revenue

If the ratio is higher, it is considered better because it suggests that a company is efficient in its operations and is good at turning sales into profits. Operating margin serves as a good indicator of how well a company is managed. It shows the amount of revenue available to cover non-operating costs, explaining why investors, analysts, and lenders pay close attention to it.

If the operating margin is highly variable, it tells you how risky the business is. By taking a close look at a company's past operating margin, you can measure its performance and tell whether it has been doing well or not. To improve the operating margin, one must ensure better management controls, improved pricing, efficient resource mobilization, and effective marketing.

Let us consider an example;

If a company has revenues of $1 million, administrative expenses of $250,000, and COGS of $350,000, its operating earnings would be [$1 million − ($250,000+$350,000)], which equals $400,000. In that case, the operating margin would be ($400,000/$1 million), which equals 40%. However, if a company negotiates better prices with its suppliers to significantly lower the COGS to $250,000, there will be a significant improvement in its operating margin to 50%.

That said, operating margin must only be used in comparing companies operating in the same sector because, ideally, they have similar business models and annual sales. However, suppose the companies are in different sectors. In that case, their business models and annual sales are wildly different, and comparing their operating margin is only meaningless – It's like comparing apples and oranges.

Return on assets (ROA)

This indicates how profitable a company is relative to its total assets. This metric offers analysts, managers, and investors an idea of how efficient a company's management is to generate income and use assets. It is considered that the higher the ROA, the better.

Think about it – every business is about efficiency – making the most of limited resources. By comparing profits to revenue, you can tell so much about a business's operations. To calculate ROA, use the formula;

ROA = A company's net income / Total assets

The higher the ROA, the better; it suggests that the company is more asset-efficient.

Let us consider an example;

Samuel and Peter both start a grocery store. Samuel spends $3,000 on his container stall, while Peter spends $30,000 on his grocery store in a mega mall. Assuming these are the only assets each investor deployed if, over a duration, Samuel earns $300 while Peter earns $2,400. This would mean Peter has a more valuable business. But Samuel would have a more efficient business. This is because Peter's ROA would be $2400/$30000, which equals 8%. Samuel's ROA would be $300/$3000, which equals 10%.

Return on equity

This financial performance measure is obtained by dividing net income by shareholder equity. Considering shareholder equity is equal to a company's assets less the debt, ROE stands for the return on net assets. This metric is considered a measure of a company's profitability with stockholder's equity.

To calculate ROE, use the formula;

ROE = Net income / Average shareholders' equity

Here, the net income is the amount of income, taxes, and net taxes a company generates over a specified duration. On the other hand, shareholders' equity is the sum of equity at the start of the duration. The start and end of the duration must coincide with the period the company earns net income. The net income and shareholder's equity are on the income statement and balance sheet, respectively.

It is best to calculate ROE based on average equity over time because of the balance sheet and income statements mismatch. That said, what is considered normal among stock peers determines whether the ROE is good or bad. The rule of thumb is to work towards an ROE equal to or above the average of peer groups.

Realize that a high ROE might not always be a good thing because it could suggest many issues like excessive debt or inconsistent profits. On the other hand, a negative ROE due to net loss or negative shareholder equity may not be used to analyse the company, nor can it compare it to companies with a positive ROE.

PART 3: BEHIND
THE SCENES

INCOME STATEMENT (statement of operations)

This is one of the three important financial statements used by a company to report its financial performance over a specific period. It is also termed as the profit and loss statement. Its primary focus is on its revenues and expenses over a particular duration. The income statement offers a deeper insight into a company's operations, efficiency of its management, and underperforming sectors relative to other industry peers.

The income statement must be submitted to the Securities and Exchange Commission (SEC). There are four key areas the income statement focuses on;

- Revenue
- Expenses
- Profits x Losses

However, it does not differentiate between cash and non-cash receipts. Instead, it starts with sale details and works down to calculate the net income and earnings per share (EPS). In short, it accounts for a company's net revenue generated and how it is transformed into net earnings – profits or losses. On the income statement, these details are shown;

Operating revenue is the revenue generated through the company's primary activities. If a company is manufacturing products, distributing, or retailing, the revenue derived from its primary activities is obtained from the sale of its products. Similarly, for a service business, revenue is the money drawn from the company's primary activities or earned through the exchange of offering those services.

Non-operating revenue – is the revenue obtained through secondary, non-core business activities. In other words, they are sourced from activities outside the purchase and sale of goods and services. They include the capital lying in the bank, rental income from company property, income from advertisement display set on a company's property.

Profits/gains – refers to the money earned from other activities like the sale of long-term assets. This could be gotten from selling old transportation vans, unused land, or subsidiary companies.

That said, revenue must not be confused with receipts. You must note that revenue is accounted for in the period when sales are made, or services are delivered.

- Expenses and losses – refer to the cost of a business continuing its operations and turning profits. Some of the company's expenses may be written off on a tax return and must meet the guidelines given by the IRS.
- The primary activity expenses are all expenses incurred to earn the normal operating revenue associated with the business's core activities. Some of the items that make up this list include employee wages, utility expenses, and sales commissions.
- The secondary activity expenses are all non-core business activities – including interest paid on loan.
- Losses are all expenses incurred on the loss-making sale of long-term assets, unusual costs, or one-time expenses.

Revenue

This refers to the income generated from running a normal business operation. It includes the discounts and deductions made on returned merchandise. In short, it is the top-of-the-line income figure from which we subtract costs in determining the net income.

Revenue = Sales price x Number of units sold

On an income statement, revenue is termed as sales. If you run a startup business, you must make positive revenue as early as possible. Revenue is also called the price-to-sales ratio. In most cases, revenue is the top line because it appears as the first thing on an income statement. On the other hand, net income is considered the bottom line because it is revenue-less expenses. When revenue exceeds expenses, it means a company is making profits.

A company's revenue can be classified into various divisions. For instance, a company can have different divisions that serve as a separate source of revenue. It can also be divided into operating revenue derived from a company's core business and non-operating revenue obtained from secondary sources. The non-operating revenues are often non-recurring and unpredictable – often one-time gains.

In real estate investment, revenue is the income generated from property – like parking fees, rent, or even on-site laundry costs. In non-profit organizations, revenue is the gross receipts – like donations from foundations, individuals, or companies. In the case of governments, revenue is the money obtained through taxation, fines, fees, sale of securities, minerals, or intergovernmental grants.

Cost and expenses

Cost means that you have expended resources to acquire something, take to a location, and set it up. However, it doesn't necessarily mean that the items you have acquired have been consumed. Until an expended resource has been consumed, it is an asset.

Let us consider an example;

To acquire an automobile, you need to pay $40,000 –the cost of acquisition – which is likely to include sale taxes and delivery charges. If you are building a product, the total expenditure you used in building it – including materials, manufacturing overhead, and labor – is cost.

On the other hand, an expense refers to a cost whose utility has been consumed. For instance, the automobile you just purchased for $40,000 will be charged to expense through depreciation over time, while the product you created will be charged to the cost of goods and services sold when it is eventually sold.

The other way you can think of an expense is any expenditure made to generate revenue. As soon as any related revenue is recognized, the cost is converted into an expense. In other words, the difference between cost and expense is that cost identifies expenditure, while an expense suggests consumption of the acquired item. Most people treat the cost as an expense because most expenditure is consumed immediately.

Depreciation and amortization

Depreciation refers to the expensing of a fixed asset over its lifetime. Realize that fixed assets are tangible – like equipment, vehicles, buildings, office furniture, machinery, or land. Considering tangible assets might have some value at the end of their life, you can calculate depreciation by subtracting its salvage value from the original cost. The difference is what depreciates evenly over the years. The amount of depreciation that happens annually is considered a tax deduction for the company until the useful life of an asset is expired.

For instance, a company can use an office building before rundown or sell for many years. In that case, the cost of building is spread out over the building's predicted lifetime, with a fraction of that cost being expensed in every accounting year.

Amortization is the practice of spreading the cost of an intangible asset – like trademarks and patents, organizational cost, franchise agreement, or proprietary processes, etc. – over its useful life.

Unlike depreciation, this is expensed on a straight-line basis. In other words, a similar amount is expensed in every period over an asset's useful life; and the assets expensed this way don't have resale or salvage value.

Total cost

The total cost is the sum of variable and fixed costs of a batch of goods or services. To obtain the total cost, you can use the following formula;

Total cost = (Average variable cost + Average fixed cost) x number of units sold

Let us consider an example;

Suppose a company incurs $20,000 of fixed cost to produce 1,000 units. Then the average fixed cost per unit is ($20,000/1000 units), which equals $20 per unit. If the variable cost per unit is $4, the total cost at the end of the production of 1,000 units would be ($20 + $ 4) x 1,000 units, which equals $24,000.

That said, the total cost is accompanied by many limitations;

There is a limited range for average fixed cost
Variable purchasing costs are based on volume. Direct labor is fixed, and yet it is not considered this way.

To correct these issues, you must recalculate the total cost whenever there is a change in the unit volume by a significant amount.

Income (loss) from continuing operations

First, we must understand that continuing operations refer to all business operations, excluding any segments that have been discontinued. These operations generate revenue through sales, which is reported in a multi-step income statement. Therefore, income from continuing business operations refers to company earnings after deducting expenses. If this value is positive, then the business is making profits. However, if the value is negative, the business is making losses.

To calculate the income from continuing operations, you subtract the cost of goods sold and other operating expenses. Let us consider an example;

If a company reports $360,000 of sales, $160,000 cost of sold goods, and $30,000 of operating expenses, then the income from operations will be ($360,000 – ($160,000+$30,000)), which equals $170,000.

That said, when calculating the income from operations, you must exclude earned/paid interest and taxes. You must not include any gains or losses derived from irregular business activities like sales or purchase of business assets.

Income or loss from operations must not be confused with net income. This is mainly because net income includes the income from continuing operations, income from discontinued operations, and unusual or irregular income. However, the income from continuing operations accounts for the revenue generated from regular business activities only. Recognizing this difference offers insight into the company's profitability.

Net income (loss) from continuing operations

A line item on the income statement detailing the after-tax earnings a business generates from its operational activities is the net income from continuing operation. Considering that discontinued operations and other one-time events are excluded, the net income from continuing operations is considered a key indicator of a company's financial health.

Net Loss

You get a net loss when expenses exceed income or total revenue generated over a given duration. Net loss is often referred to as a net operating loss (NOL). Realize that companies that incur a net loss are not necessarily declared bankrupt because they may choose to use their retained earnings or take a loan to stay afloat. However, this strategy is only short-term because a company that is not profitable will not survive long term.

Think of the net loss as a company's bottom line. To calculate net loss, use the following formula;

Net profit or net loss = Revenues generated – Expenses incurred

Considering revenues and expenses are matched over a given duration, a net loss is considered an example of the matching principle – an integral component of the accrual accounting technique. Any expenses related to the income earned over a given duration are included/matched to that duration irrespective of when they are paid.

When the profits decline below the expenses and cost of goods sold, it results in a net loss. However, if the profits go above the expenses and cost of goods sold, it results in a net profit.

In short, low revenues contribute to net losses. Some of the revenues that contribute to low revenues include; unsuccessful marketing strategies, stiff competition, inefficient marketing staff, not keeping up with the market demands, or even weak pricing strategies. When the revenue is low, it translates to low profits, and when the profits fall below the expenses and COGS over a given duration, it results in net losses.

Let us consider an example; if company A makes $250,000 in sales, and has $190,000 in COGS, and $130,000 in expenses, then it makes a gross profit of ($250,000-$190,000)=$60,000. However, the expenses exceed the gross profit; hence the company makes a net loss of $70,000.

Net income attributable to

Net income attributable to shareholders refers to one step down from the net income reflected in the income statement. Remember, a company's net income refers to all the revenues a company generates fewer expenses, including taxes and interest expenses. Therefore, the net income attributable to shareholders is less noncontrolling interests – also called minority interests.

Earnings (loss) per share attributable to and diluted EPS

This is a company's net profit divided by outstanding common shares. The resulting figure tells us whether the company is making profits or losses. The higher the EPS, the more profitable a company is, and vice versa. In other words, EPS tells us how much money a company is making per share of its stock; hence widely used as a metric for estimating the value of a company.

Investors are likely to pay more for its shares when the EPS value is high, especially if they think that the company has higher profits relative to the share price. To calculate the EPS, use the following formula;

Earnings per share = (Net income – Preferred dividends) / End of-period common shares outstanding

EPS is one of the most important indicators when picking stocks. If you are interested in stock trading or investing, choosing a broker that matches your investment style is next. Realize that comparing EPS in absolute terms may not be meaningful because an ordinary shareholder doesn't have direct access to the earnings. The trick is to compare EPS with the stock share price when determining the value of earnings and how you feel about the company's future growth.

Conversely, diluted earnings per share serve as a key metric in conducting fundamental analysis to measure the quality of a company's EPS – assuming that all convertible securities – outstanding convertible shares, equity options, convertible debts, and warrants – have been exercised.

To calculate the diluted EPS, use the following formula;

Diluted EPS = (Net income – preferred dividends) / (WASO+CDS)

Where:

WASO is the weighted average shares outstanding
CDS is the conversion of the dilutive securities

You must note that dilutive securities are not common stock but securities that can be converted to common stock. When you convert these securities, the EPS declines; hence, the diluted EPS tends always to be lower than EPS. In other words, diluted EPS serves as a conservative metric indicating a worst-case scenario concerning EPS. This is because a diluted EPS considers what would happen in case dilutive securities were exercised. For instance, if they increased the weighted number of shares outstanding, there would be a decline in the EPS.

Let us consider an example;

An ABC company had $100 million in net income over the past year. However, the company did not pay any dividends. Assuming a company has $30 million common shares. The company also has employee stock options, which could be converted to $2 million common shares, and convertible preferred shares that could be converted to $6 million common shares. The resulting diluted EPS would be;

[($100 million - $0) / ($30 million + $2 million + $6 million)] = $2.63/share.

On the other hand, the basic EPS would be;

[($100 million -$0) / $30 million)] = $3.33

If the company has convertible securities, the diluted EPS is less than its basic EPS.

BALANCE SHEET

Assets

This is a resource that possesses an economic value. An individual, country, or company controls or owns, anticipating that it will offer benefits in the future. Assets are reported on a balance sheet and are created or bought to increase the value of a company and benefit its operations. Think of an asset as something that in the future promises to generate cash flow, lower expenses, and boost sales.

For a company to possess assets, it must have its rights as of the date of its financial statements. Realize that an economic resource is scarce and can benefit by lowering cash outflows and increasing cash inflows. Assets are classified into various categories;

- Current assets
- Financial investments
- Fixed assets
- Intangible assets

Current assets are also termed short-term assets. They are economic resources anticipated for conversion into cash within a year. They include cash and cash equivalents, inventory, accounts receivable, and other prepaid expenses.

Fixed assets refer to long-term resources like buildings, equipment, and plants. For a fixed asset, an adjustment for aging is made based on periodic charges called depreciation. According to generally accepted accounting principles (GAAP), depreciation happens in two ways. We have the straight-line method, which assumes that the rate at which a fixed asset loses its value is directly proportional to its useful life. And we also have the accelerated method, which assumes that a fixed asset loses its value faster during its initial years of use.

Financial assets are investments in assets and securities of other companies. They include sovereign and corporate bonds, stocks, preferred equity, and other hybrid securities. They are valued based on how an investment is classified, and its motive.

Finally, intangible assets are resources that don't have a physical presence – like trademarks, patents, goodwill, and copyrights. Accounting for these assets varies depending on the type of asset, and they can be amortized or tested for annual impairment.

Current assets

These are all assets a company expects to be conveniently consumed, sold, used, or exhausted through standard business operations within a year. They appear on a company's balance sheet. They include cash and cash equivalents, inventory, accounts receivable, current accounts, and other prepaid expenses.

The importance of current assets to companies is that they are used to fund daily business operations and pay outgoing operating expenses. Considering this is reported as a dollar value of all assets and resources easily convertible to cash in a short duration, it also represents a company's liquid assets.

That said, you must exercise caution to include only qualifying assets capable of liquidation at a fair price over the next year. For example, there is a high chance that fast-moving consumer goods produced by a company can be sold easily over the next year. While inventory is included in the current assets, it may be challenging to sell heavy machinery or land, so they are excluded from the current assets.

Depending on the nature of the business and its products, current assets can be anything from barrels of crude oil, work-in-progress inventory, fabricated goods, foreign currency, or raw materials.

Accounts receivable refer to the money due to a company for delivery of goods and services; or used but not yet paid for by clients as long as they are expected to be paid within a year. Therefore, if a company offers long-term credits to its clients, a fraction of its accounts receivable may not be included in the current assets. There is also a possibility that some accounts may never be settled in full.

Inventory refers to the finished products, raw materials, and other components. That said, its consideration may require more careful thought. Different accounting methods can inflate the inventory and may not be as liquid as other current assets based on the industry sector or product in question.

Prepaid expenses refer to advance payments a company makes for goods and services expected to be received in the future. While these expenses may not be converted to cash, they are considered payments already made to free up the capital for other uses. They include contractors and insurance payments. Current assets are displayed in order of liquidity on the balance sheet, with those highly likely to be converted into cash ranked higher. To calculate current assets, use the formula;

Current assets = C + CE + I + AR + MS + PE + OLA

Where;

- C = Cash
- CE = Cash Equivalents
- I = Inventory
- AR = Accounts Receivable
- MS = Marketable Securities
- PE = Prepaid Expenses
- OLA = Other Liquid Assets

Let us consider an example; A leading retail company's total current assets for the fiscal year ending March 2020 is a sum of $8 billion cash, $6.2 billion accounts receivable, $47.25 billion inventory, and $4.23 billion other current assets. The total current assets are ($8 billion+$6.2 billion+$47.25 billion+$4.23 billion), which equals $65.68 billion.

Cash and cash equivalents

This line item on the balance sheet reports the value of a company's assets by looking at its cash or those convertible into cash immediately. Cash equivalents include treasury bills, commercial paper, and short-term government bonds, and other marketable securities with maturities of less than 90 days and bank accounts. Often, cash equivalents don't include stock holdings or equity because they tend to fluctuate in value.

The good thing about cash and cash equivalents is that they help companies with their needs for working capital, considering they can be used to pay off current liabilities like short-term debts and bills.

Cash is money that is in the form of currency. They include coins, bills, and currency notes. Some companies hold more than one currency, hence likely to experience currency exchange risk. Any foreign currency must be translated to the reporting currency for financial reporting reasons. The results obtained from these conversions must be comparable to those that would have been obtained if the business had completed operations using one currency only. That said, translation losses from the devaluation of a foreign currency are not reported with the cash and cash equivalents. Stead are reported in accumulated other comprehensive income categories.

Cash equivalents refer to investments readily convertible to cash. These investments are often short-term, with a maximum investment period of 90 days or less. If the investment matures in more than 90 days, it is classified under other investments. Cash equivalents are highly liquid and easily sold in the market, making their buyers easily accessible.

That said, all-cash equivalents must have known market price and must not be subject to price fluctuations. Their value must not be expected to change significantly before maturity or redemption. Depending on their maturity date, certificates of deposit may be considered. Like most people think, cash and cash equivalents don't include credit collateral or inventory.

Receivables

They are also referred to as accounts receivable. They are debts owed to a company's clients for delivered or used but not yet paid goods and services. Receivables are created by extending a customer's line of credit and reported as current assets on the balance sheet. Considering they can be used as collateral in securing a loan for one to meet their short-term obligations, they can be considered as liquid assets.

Additionally, receivables are considered as part of a company's working capital. Effectively managing receivables involves follow-ups with clients who have not paid and then discussing potential payment plan arrangements where necessary. This is critical in providing extra capital to support operations and lower net debts.

To improve their cash flows, they must reduce their credit terms for their receivable accounts. This way, their cash conversion cycle is reduced. The company may also sell receivables at a discount to a factoring company, which takes over responsibility for collecting money owed and takes on the risk by default – an arrangement termed as accounts receivable financing.

To measure how effective a company is at extending credit and collecting debt on that credit, analysts focus on many ratios;

- *Receivable turnover ratio*, which is the net value of credit sales over a given duration divided by the average accounts receivable – the sum of the value of accounts receivable at the beginning of the desired period to the value at the end of the period; divided by two – during that same duration.
- *Days sales outstanding (DSO)* is the average number of days it takes for payments to be collected after a sale has been made.

Inventories

This is a term used to describe the available goods for sale and the raw materials used to produce those goods. An inventory represents the most important asset because its turnover is the primary source of revenue generation and the subsequent earnings for its shareholders. It serves as a buffer between manufacturing and fulfillment of orders.

The mistake most businesses make is holding an inventory for long durations. This is mainly because of storage costs and the threat of obsolescence. That said, inventory can be valued in three ways;

- *The first-in, first-out method (FIFO)* which suggests that the cost of sold goods is based on the cost of the materials purchased earlier, while the remaining inventory is based on the materials purchased last.
- *The last-in, first-out method (LIFO)* suggests that the cost of sold goods is valued by looking at the cost of the last materials purchased. In contrast, the value of the remaining inventory is based on materials purchased earliest.
- *The weighted average method*, which requires valuing both the inventory and the cost of goods sold, should be based on the average cost of all materials purchased during that period.

Inventories are classified into three:

  - Raw materials – the unprocessed materials used in the production process like steel and aluminum in car manufacturing, crude oil for oil refineries, or flour for bakeries.

  - Work-in progress – the partially processed goods waiting for completion or resale. It is also termed as inventory on the production floor. They include half-assembled cars or airliners, etc.

- Finished goods – the complete products ready for sale. Typically, this is merchandise such as clothes, electronics, or cars.

Other current assets

This is a class of valuable things a company owns, benefits from, or uses to generate revenue that is convertible to cash within a business cycle. They are referred to as "other" because they are insignificant or uncommon, unlike typical current assets. OCA accounts are listed as components of a company's total assets in a balance sheet.

At times, a one-off situation in a company's 10-K filings results in recognizing other current assets. Because of these assets, the net balance in the OCA account is typically small. OCAs include restricted cash or investments, advances paid to employees or suppliers, cash surrender value of life insurance policies, or a piece of property being prepared for sale.

Let us consider an example – for a company's quarter ending May 31, 2020, the recorded total asset on its balance sheet was $276.82 billion. Of this total, 62% were attributed to current assets. Other current assets made up a small fraction of $135.23 billion of the current assets. These assets were listed at $7.80 billion, which accounts for about 4% of the company's liquid assets.

Intangible assets

This is an asset that is not physical – like intellectual property, goodwill, or recognition. These assets exist in opposition to tangible assets like vehicles, inventory, or equipment.

Intangible assets can either be definite or indefinite. For instance, a company's brand name is considered an indefinite intangible asset considering it stays with the company as long as it's in operation. On the other hand, an example of a definite intangible asset is a legal agreement to operate under another company's patent without extending the agreement. In this case, the agreement has a limited life, hence a definite asset.

While intangible assets don't have the obvious physical value, it proves valuable and critical to their long-term success or failure. For instance, Coca-Cola wouldn't be nearly as successful if not for the money generated through brand recognition. While brand recognition is not a physical asset – seen or touched – it has a meaningful impact on sales generation.

The good news is that companies can create or acquire intangible assets and write off their expenses in the process – like hiring a lawyer or filing a patent application. Additionally, all the expenses incurred in creating the intangible asset are expensed. That said, these expenses don't appear on the balance sheet, and there are no records of their book value. Because of this, when a company is sold, the purchase price is likely to be above the book value of the assets reflected in the balance sheet.

Total assets

These are the total assets owned by a person or an entity. They are of economic value and are expended over time to benefit the owner. If a business owns them, they are recorded in the accounting records and its balance sheet. Typically, you will find them in various categories like cash, inventory, prepaid expenses, marketable securities, goodwill, intangible assets, among other assets.

Based on the accounting standards applicable, assets that comprise total assets may or may not be recorded at their current market values. Generally, the international financial reporting standards are amenable to stating the assets at their current market values, while GAAP is less likely to accommodate these restatements.

Most owners look at their assets concerning being converted to cash fast. An asset is more liquid if it can be sold readily to cash. A potential buyer will focus on various types of assets listed on a company's balance sheet, emphasizing whether the asset's value on the balance sheet corresponds to the actual value of the asset. If they find that the actual value is lower, they are likely to lower the size of their bid. However, if the asset's value is higher, they will be more interested in acquiring the business and likely increase their offer price.

Liability

This is something – usually money – that an individual or company owes. Liabilities are often settled over duration through the transfer of money, goods, or services. You will find liabilities listed on a company's right side of a balance sheet – like mortgages, loans, warranties, deferred revenues, accounts payable, or bonds.

Typically, a liability acts as an obligation between one party and another not yet paid for. Liabilities are classified into two;

- Current liabilities
- Non-current
  liabilities

Liabilities are considered critical for a company because they are used to paying for large expansions or running financial operations. They also make transactions between the company and other businesses more efficient. For instance, if a winery sells wine to a restaurant, it doesn't demand payment upon delivery of wine. However, the restaurant invoices the winery to make drop-off efficient and paying easier. Here, the outstanding payment the restaurant owes the winery is considered a liability. On the other hand, the winery considers this amount owed an asset.

Current liabilities

These are a company's short-term financial obligations due within a year or within a normal cycle of operations – also known as the cash conversion cycle, which is the time it takes a company to purchase inventory and then convert sales into cash. A good example of a current liability is money owed in the form of accounts payable.

Typically, current liabilities are settled using current assets like accounts receivable or cash. The ratio of current assets to current liabilities is critical in determining a company's continuing ability to pay off debts as they are due.

One of the largest current liability accounts is accounts payable, representing unpaid supplier invoices. Most companies try matching payment dates for accounts payable to collect their accounts receivable before due.

For instance, a company might have a 90-day term for money owed to their suppliers. This means they require their clients to pay debts within the 90-day term. Similarly, current liabilities must be settled by creating a new liability like a new short-term debt obligation.

Current liability accounts tend to vary from one company to another across industry sectors and based on the government's regulations. Most analysts and creditors use the current ratio to measure their ability to pay their short-term financial debts or obligations. This tells how well a company manages its balance sheet, especially when settling short-term debts and payables. Additionally, this ratio helps investors and analysts know whether a company has adequate current assets on its balance sheet to pay off or satisfy its current debt, among other payables.

Once a company determines it received an economic benefit that needs to be paid within a year, it must record credit entry immediately.

Based on a company's received benefits, an accountant must categorize it as an expense or asset to receive a debit entry.

Let us consider an example; a large electronics manufacturer receives a shipment of audio speakers from its vendors with whom it must pay $20 million within 60 days. Considering these materials are not placed into production immediately, the company's accounting office records a credit entry to accounts payable and debits entry to inventory, an asset account for $20 million. Once the company settles the balance due to suppliers, it debits accounts payable and credit cash for $20 million.

Accounts payable

This is an account in the general ledger representing a company's obligation to pay off a short-term debt to its suppliers. It also refers to a company's division or department responsible for paying its suppliers and other creditors. The total accounts payable appears under current liabilities in the balance sheet, mainly because they are debts that must be settled within a specified duration without fail.

At the corporate level, accounts payable are short-term debt payments due to suppliers. In other words, it is an IOU from one company to another. In that case, the other entity would record the transaction as an increase to the accounts receivable in the same figures.

The accounts payable are important figures in a company's balance sheet. If it increases over a prior duration, the company purchases more goods or services on credit instead of making cash payments. On the contrary, if the accounts payable decrease, the company is paying on its previous period debts faster than it is purchasing new items on credit.

In other words, accounts payable is a company's way of knowing how it manages its cash flow. If using an indirect method in preparing cash flow statements, a net increase or decrease in accounts payable from the previous period must appear in the top section as the cash flow from operating activities. In that case, a company's management can use accounts payable to manipulate its cash flow to a certain degree.

For instance, if the company wants to increase their cash reserves for a given duration, they may opt to extend the business's time to pay all outstanding accounts in accounts payable. However, this payment flexibility must be weighed against the relationship between the company and its vendors. Good business practice requires payment of bills by their due dates.

Other long-term liabilities

This line item lumps together obligations not due within a year on a balance sheet. The difference between this and other liabilities is that they are less urgent to repay but are classified as "other" because a company doesn't see them as important enough to warrant individual identification.

While they are liabilities – meaning debts a company owes, long-term liabilities are not urgent for at least 12 months or defined as its operating cycle. Some companies choose to disclose the composition in their footnotes to financial statements if they think it can be used as material.

Examples of other long-term liabilities include; pension liabilities, capital leases, deferred credits, customer deposits, and deferred tax liabilities. If it is a holding company, it will have intercompany borrowings, loans made from one company division to another.

Equity

Typically, this is also referred to as shareholders' equity. It is the money that would be returned to a company's shareholders if all assets were liquidated and all the company's debt was paid off in liquidation. In acquisition, the value of a company's sale is fewer liabilities owed by the company but not transferred with the sale. Additionally, it can represent a company's book value. Sometimes, equity is offered as a payment-in-kind.

To calculate equity, simply use the following formula;

Shareholder's Equity=Total Assets-Total Liabilities

This information is present on the balance sheet, where these steps must be followed;

- First, locate a company's total assets for the first period
- Secondly, locate the total liabilities listed separately on the balance sheet
- Thirdly, find the difference between total assets and total liabilities to obtain the shareholders' equity
- Finally, note that the total assets equal the sum of liabilities and total equity

Shareholders' equity can also be expressed as retained earnings and share capital with fewer treasury shares' values. However, this method is not commonly used. Although both methods give the same figure, total liabilities and total assets are more illustrative of a company's financial health.

Retained earnings

This is a key concept in accounting that refers to historical profits earned by a company fewer dividends it paid in the past. The term "*retained*" suggests that because these earnings were not paid out to shareholders as dividends, they were retained by the company instead. Because of this, retained earnings decline when it loses money or when it pays dividends and rise when net profits are generated. Profits allow the company to use the surplus money earned – by paying shareholders or reinvesting it back into the business for growth and expansion.

$$RE = BP + \text{net income (or loss)} - c - s$$

Where:

- BP=Beginning Period RE
- C=Cash dividends
- S=Stock dividends

When retained earnings are expressed as a percentage of total earnings, it is termed retention ratio, which equals (1 – dividend payout ratio). Although the last option of debt repayment leads to money leaving the business, it still has a great impact on the company's business account – like saving for the future interest payments

Total equity

This is the difference between assets and liabilities. Total equity is often found on a company's balance sheet. Some asset line items include cash, marketable securities, accounts receivable, prepaid expenses, inventory, fixed assets, goodwill, and other assets. On the other hand, the liability items to be aggregated include; accounts payable, accrued liabilities, short-term debts, unearned revenue, long-term debt, and other liabilities.

To calculate the total equity, use the following formula;

Total equity = Assets – Liabilities

Therefore, every asset and liability item listed on the balance sheet must be included in calculating total equity. That said, there is an alternative approach for calculating equity by summing all the line items in the shareholders' equity section of the balance sheet – like retained earnings, common stock, additional paid-in capital, less treasury stock.

Essentially, total equity refers to the amount investors invest in a company in exchange for stocks, including all subsequent business earnings but less all subsequent dividends paid out. Most smaller businesses are strapped for cash and have never paid a dividend, meaning that total equity is the sum of invested funds and all subsequent earnings.

Let us consider an example;

The balance sheet of company XYZ contains a total asset value of $1 million and total liabilities of $600,000. Total equity is ($1 million - $600,000), which equals $400,000.

Lenders can use the derived amount to determine whether there are enough funds invested in the company to offset its debt. For investors, this amount is used to determine whether adequate equity is piled up to press for dividends. Finally, a supplier would use this amount to warrant being given credit.

CASH FLOW

C ash flow refers to the net amount of cash and cash equivalents that are moved in and out of business. The cash received by the company is termed inflow, while that spent is termed outflow. A company's cash flow is reflected on its cash flow statement, which measures the amount of cash generated or spent over a given duration.

The cash flow statement has three major sections:

- Cash flow from operations (CFO) shows the amount of cash a company brings from its regular operations or business activities. This includes amortization, accounts receivable, depreciation, accounts payable, and other items.
- Cash flow from investing (CFI) shows a company's sales and purchases of capital assets. It is the aggregate change in the business' cash position because of losses or profits derived from investments in such things as equipment or plant.
- Cash flow from financing activities (CFF) measures cash flow from one company to another or its investors, owners, or creditors. It also shows the net flow of money used in running the business, including dividends, equity, and debt.

Cash provided by operations

This refers to the amount of money a company brings in from ongoing business operations like manufacturing or selling goods and services. It does not include capital expenditure, expense, or investment revenue. The finance officers focus mainly on the core business, referred to as net cash from operating activities or operating cash flow (OCF).

Cash flow accounts for the total amount of money transferred into and out of business. Considering this affects a company's liquidity, it allows the owners and operators to check where the money is going and where it is coming from. It also helps them develop the necessary strategies to help them generate and maintain steady cash flow for efficient business operations and financing decisions.

A company's cash flow details are found in the cash flow statements, which are part of a company's annual and quarterly reports. If the cash flow from operating activities is positive, the core business activities are thriving. It also offers additional potential for profitability.

Investors are interested in the cash flow from operating activities to determine where a company is getting its money from. There are two ways the cash flow from operating activities is displayed on a cash flow statement;

Indirect method – where the company starts with the net income on an accrual accounting basis and then works backwards to obtain the cash basis figure for that duration. Here, revenue is recognized when earned and not necessarily when cash is received.

Let us consider an example;

If a customer purchases a widget on credit at $1000, the sale has been made, but no cash has been received. Here, the revenue is still recognized in that sale month, and it will be shown in the company's net income statement as part of its net income. In that case, the net income is overstated by $1000 on a cash basis. Once this amount is offset, it appears as part of accounts receivable on the balance sheet.

Direct method – A company records all transactions on a cash basis. The information is shown on the cash flow statement using actual cash inflows and outflows during the accounting period. The direct method examples of cash flows from operating activities include salaries paid to employees, cash paid to vendors and suppliers, cash collected from customers, interest income and dividends received, and income tax paid and interest paid.

Of the two methods, most accountants prefer the indirect method for its simplicity in preparing the cash flow statements by deriving information from the company's balance sheet and income statements. However, the financial accounting standard board (FASB) prefers the direct method to give a clearer picture of the cash flowing in and out of business.

To calculate cash flow from operating activities, use this formula;

Cash Flow from Operating Activities = Funds from Operations + Changes in Working Capital

This is where funds from operations are the sum of net income, depletion, depreciation, amortization, investment tax credit, deferred taxes, and other funds.

Let us consider an example;

The cash flow details from a leading technology company for the fiscal year ended November 2020 had a net worth of $60.34 billion. Depreciation, Depletion, & Amortization was $13.3 billion, Deferred Taxes & Investment Tax Credit of -$23.43 billion, and Other Funds of $6.7 billion. Using the indirect formula, the summation of this gives $56.91 billion. The net change in working capital for that period was $23.76 billion. If you add it to the funds from operations, you get the cash flow from operating activities to be $80.67.

Cash used in investing activities

This is one of the sections on a cash flow statement that reports how much cash has been created or spent from various investment-related activities – purchases of physical assets, investing in securities, or the sale of securities or assets – for a given duration.

If the cash flow figure is negative, the company is performing poorly. However, a negative cash flow from investing activities indicates that a large amount of cash is invested in the long-term health of a company – like research and development.

Examples of operating activities include any spending or cash sources involved in a company's daily activities. Cash flows from investing activities account for the cash used to purchase non-current assets or long-term assets that are expected to deliver value in the future.

Like any financial statement analysis, the trick is to analyze the cash flow statement in tandem with the balance sheet and income statements to give a full picture of a company's financial wellbeing.

Borrowing base

This refers to how much money a lender is willing to loan a company. It is often based on the value of the collateral the company pledges. To obtain the borrowing base, "margining" is done by determining a discount factor multiplied by the collateral value in question. The figure represents the amount of money a lender will loan out to the company.

Some of the assets that can be used as collateral include accounts receivable, inventory, and equipment. If a company borrows money from a lender, the lender assesses the company's strengths and weaknesses. The lender associates it with loaning money to this company depending on the perceived risk. In that case, a discount factor can be determined—say 80%. Considering the discount factor, if the borrower offers $250,000 worth of collateral, the maximum cash the lender will give the company is 80% of $250,000, which equals $200,000.

You must note that a lender is more comfortable giving a loan rooted in borrowing bases because they are made against specific sets of assets. Moreover, the borrowing base is adjustable downward to protect the lender. For instance, a decline in the collateral value means a decline in the credit limit. Alternatively, the borrowing base will increase to a predetermined limit should the collateral value rise.

Dividends

This is the distribution of a company's earnings to its shareholders' class as determined by its board of directors. Typically, the common shareholders are eligible as long as they own the stock before the ex-dividend date. Dividends may be paid out as cash or in additional stock.

The shareholders must approve dividends through their voting rights. While cash dividends are the most common, dividends can be issued as shares of stock or other property. It is considered a token reward paid to its shareholders for investing in a company's equity, and it typically comes from the company's net profits.

Considering a good fraction of the company's profits as retained earnings, the remainder can be given to shareholders in the form of dividends. In other cases, a company may still give dividends even though they are not making suitable profits for the sake of maintaining their established track record of making regular dividend payments.

Dividend payments tend to follow a chronological order of events, and the dates are used to tell which shareholder qualifies to receive dividend payments. For instance;

- The announcement dates are when dividends are announced by company management and must be approved by the shareholders before they can be paid.
- Ex-dividend date is when the dividend eligibility expires. Here, the shareholders who buy the stock on or after this date don't qualify to receive dividends.
- The record date determines which shareholders are eligible for a dividend.
- The Payment date is when money is credited to investors' accounts.

Companies pay dividends for many reasons, with different implications and interpretations for investors. It can be viewed as a reward to investors for their trust in a company. In that case, a company honors this sentiment by delivering a strong track record of dividend payments.

Most shareholders prefer dividend payments because they are treated as tax-free income in many countries. Conversely, a capital gain realized through the sale of a share whose price has increased is taxable income.

If the dividends are of high value, the company is doing well and has generated good profits. However, it can mean that the company does not have suitable projects to generate better income in the future, which explains why they use their cash to pay shareholders instead of reinvesting it into its growth and expansion.

If the dividend amount declines, it does not necessarily mean bad news about a company. It may mean the company has better plans for investing the money, given its financials and operations.

Reduction of borrowings

This is also termed debt reduction or debt relief. It refers to a process of reducing the debt balance by a company using a systematic approach of repayment or a financial maneuver that boosts your debtor position. The best strategies used to reduce borrowings are refinancing and reorganization of debt, making payoff more efficient.

- *Refinancing* – is a maneuver used by businesses to improve their financial position. It involves utilizing funds for a new loan to settle the existing loans. It is commonly used with mortgages to help investors get out of higher-rate and lower-rate loans. Certain refinancing options offer cash-out components that allow investors to get equity of their property or asset to pay off the high-interest borrowing.
- *Reorganizing* – refers to a formal process a business uses to avoid being declared bankrupt. While this method has drawbacks, it allows companies to manage part of their overwhelming debt load that is standing in the way of their business stability and growth.

Reduction of borrowings offers a wide range of psychological and financial benefits. First, a debt reduction makes it more feasible for a company to keep up with its monthly debt payments by avoiding delays, which risks additional fines. A lower debt balance reduces the interest paid both in the short- and long term. In turn, this adds up to a significant amount of savings.

The healthiest way to reduce borrowings is by paying it fast and efficiently. The sooner a company can pay its debt, the less risk they run if the situation gets out of control. Reduction of borrowings calls for discipline and strategic approaches that go above and beyond meeting the minimum monthly payment requirements.

Repurchases of common stock

This is also known as a share buyback.

This refers to a transaction where a company buys back its shares from the marketplace, perhaps because the management thinks they are undervalued. Alternatively, the company may offer its shareholders the option of tendering its shares directly to the company at a fixed price. This way, it lowers the number of outstanding shares and increases the demand for the shares and the price.

Considering a share repurchase reduces the number of shares outstanding, the earnings per share (EPS) increases. If the EPS is high, the market value of the remaining shares also goes up. Once they have been repurchased, they are canceled or held as treasury shares. This lowers a company's available cash, shown on the balance sheet as a significant reduction in the amount spent on buybacks. Simultaneously, the share repurchases lower shareholders' equity by an equal amount on the liabilities side of the balance sheet. Any investor interested in finding out how much a company has spent on share repurchases can examine the company's quarterly earnings reports.

The most important thing to note is that if a business pays out the same amount of money to shareholders in dividends every year, and the total shares reduce, it means every shareholder will receive a larger number of dividends annually. If the business grows its earnings and total dividend payouts, reducing the number of shares will increase the growth of dividends. A shareholder expects that a company will maintain regular dividend payouts.

The advantage of buybacks is that they raise the share price, make a company's financial statements appear stronger, and hide a slight decline in the net income. If the share repurchases lower the shares outstanding to a greater degree than a decline in net income, there is a high chance the EPS will rise regardless of a company's financial situation.

That said, buybacks are also thought to be ill-timed in most cases. In other words, a company buys back shares when it has lots of cash or when its financial health is good in the stock market. At such a time, the stock price is highly likely to be high, and the prices are likely to drop after a buyback, implying that the company is not that healthy after all.

Additionally, a share repurchase tends to give investors the impression that a company lacks other profitable opportunities for growth, which is a great issue for someone looking to generate revenue and increase profits. A company is not obligated to repurchase shares because of economic or marketplace changes because this puts it in a precarious situation if the economy were to go downtown.

Cash provided by (used in) financing activities

This is also called cash flow from financing activities (CFF). This shows the net flow of cash used to run a company. Examples of financing activities include dividends, equity, and debt. The CFF is critical in offering investors a deeper insight into its financial strength and how well its capital structure is managed.

To calculate the cash flow from financing activities, use the following formula;

CFF = CED − (CD + RP)

Where;

- CED is the cash in-flow from debt or issuing equity
- CD is the cash paid as dividends xRP is the repurchase of equity and debt

Let us consider an example;

Company ABC has the following information in the financial activities section of its cash flow statement:

Payments of dividends: $800,000 (cash outflow)
Proceeds from long-term debt: $6,000,000 (cash inflow)
Repurchase stock: $2,000,000 (cash outflow)
Payments to long-term debt: $1,000,000 (cash outflow)

The CFF = $6 million − ($2 million + $ 1 million + $800,000) = $2.2 million.

The most important point to note is that CFF will show you how a company raises cash to maintain or grow its business activities. A company's source of capital can be equity or debt. A company takes on debt by issuing bonds or taking loans from the bank. The key is to make interest payments to creditors and bondholders to compensate them for loaning their money.

If a company decides to take the equity route, it simply issues stock to investors interested in owning a company share. Other companies choose to make dividend payments to their shareholders, hence representing a cost of equity for the company. A positive cash flow from financing activities means more money flows into the company than what is spent, increasing its assets. On the other hand, if the CFF is negative, the company is servicing debt, retiring debt, paying dividends, or making stock repurchase.

For an investor, if a company turns to new debt or equity for cash frequently, it is a sign that it is not generating enough revenue. An increase in interest rate means that the debt servicing cost also increases. The key here is that an investor digs deeper into the numbers because a positive cash flow does not necessarily mean a good thing but is saddled with large debts.

Conversely, a company frequently repurchasing stock and issuing dividends when underperforming is a warning sign. It could mean that the company's management might be trying to prop up its stock price to keep investors happy when their actions negatively affect the company in the long run.

Note that any significant changes in the cash flow from financing activities should prompt any investor to look into the company's transactions. When analyzing a company's cash flow statement, you must consider every section contributing to the overall change in its cash position.

Cash equivalents

These are short-term investment securities with high credit quality and high liquidity. They are also known as cash and equivalents, one of the three asset classes in financial investing. These securities are low-risk, low-return in nature.

Cash equivalents are one of the most important indicators of a company's financial health. This tells investors whether it is good to invest in a company or not by looking at its ability to generate cash and cash equivalents. The cash equivalents tell investors whether a company can pay its bills for a short duration.

There are five major types of cash equivalents:

- Treasury bills are securities issued by the government's treasury departments, also called T-bills. When issued to companies, they essentially lend their money to the government. Typically, they are sold for a minimum of $100 to a maximum of $5 billion. They don't pay interest. Instead, they are offered at a discounted price. The T-bills yield is the difference between the purchase price and the redemption value.
- Commercial paper – is commonly used by big companies to obtain funds that help them settle their short-term debt obligations. Typically, they are issued to companies that promise to fulfil the face amount on the stated maturity date.
- Marketable securities – refer to financial assets and instruments that are readily convertible to cash. They are highly liquid because their maturities tend to happen within a year or less, and their trading rates have minimal effect on prices.
- Money market funds –are like checking accounts paying high-interest rates given by the money deposited. They offer an efficient and effective tool for companies to manage their money because they are stable compared to other funds. This fund's share price is always constant at $1/share.
- Short-term government bonds – are funds given by the government towards its projects. Typically, they are issued using the country's domestic currency. Before investing in government bonds, investors must look at political, inflation, and interest rate risks.

Restricted cash

This is money held for a specific purpose and is not available to the company's immediate or general use. In other words, it is the money not readily or freely available for the company to invest or spend.

It appears separate from cash and cash equivalent on a company's balance sheet. The main reason it is restricted is disclosed in its financial statement. Some of the reasons may include capital investment or debt reduction.

Restricted cash can be classified into two;

- Current asset, which is used up within a year
- Non-current asset, which is long-term

Typically, restricted cash appears on a company's balance sheet as "other restricted cash" or "other assets." While there are various reasons companies restrict a fraction of their cash, the two most common uses of restricted cash include:

- Capital expenditure
- Loan and debt payments

CONCLUSION

Thank you for taking the time to buy my book. I hope this book brought you the information you were looking for. I hope you share this with those close to you so that we may spread the influence and knowledge to everyone.

If you want to be an investor or executive, fundamental analysis will make a large part of your everyday life. There is no way you will be an investor without understanding the basic terminology. With the right basic terminology, you can easily look at any data expected to impact the price or perceived value of stocks and understand the information.

The key to fundamental analysis is understanding terminology. Without understanding what each term means, it can be challenging to dig through financial statements and draw conclusions. Imagine yourself in a shopping mall to help you visualize the importance of stock terminology. Stocks are the items on sale in the retail outlets. Understanding stock terminology means you can tell the difference between the different items on the shelf. The last thing you want is to be dismissed as an unreliable, emotional shopper with no inkling of the real value of the goods on sale.

Understanding the stock terminology will help you move through the stores seeking the best deals.

So, what are you still waiting for?

It's time to master the language of stocks, invest wisely, and attain your success!

Made in the USA
Middletown, DE
06 January 2022

57964849R00049